LETTERS TO MY DARLINGS

ANDREJ MUNTÉNIE

JAN. 2025

LETTERS TO MY DARLINGS

Andrej Munténie
Letters to My Darlings

Published by Spines

ISBN: 979-8-89691-407-5

For E—, of course, and for our children, for when they're older.

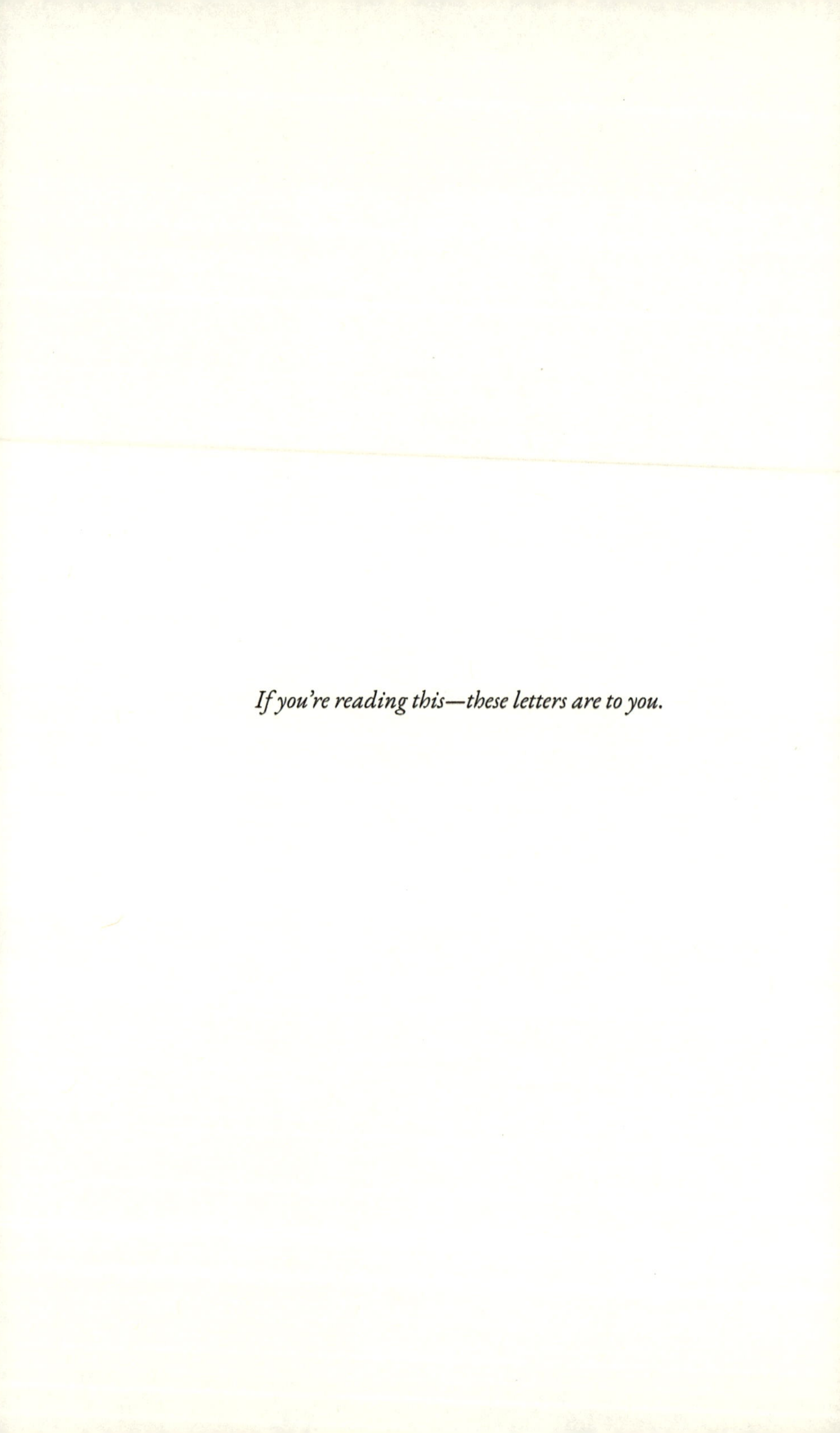

If you're reading this—these letters are to you.

I.

My dearest Y—,

Have you ever found someone who doesn't love you? Who isn't love-struck by how easy you make it, by how groovy you are?

It is my pleasure, darling, to be myself as a performance for you, to invent provocations, subversions, to wrap them in sweetness, in pleasantry, to dissect the *aesthetic quality* of what I've done, to wonder about it with you, to upset polite conversation and then with my eyes ask you, *can you believe that I...*

I've told you that I am myself in relation to you, what I mean is that in your eyes I am illuminated, what I mean is that I try to live with some sense of poetry, of imagination, of insight—and you'll watch and you'll listen, darling, won't you?

I found it so interesting when, at one of your parties, I met someone who put their hand up, just as we were in mid-conversation, to say, *excuse me, but I would be making a faux-pas if I didn't say hello to these ladies.* What a very elegant, what a very unexpected, turn of phrase— what a very elegant impulse—don't you find? Here was someone who was sensitive to poetry, to *applying the poetic as a device.* I looked for you, darling, I wanted to tell you about it.

Do you remember getting off the elevator at the Repaire Bohème, when I hugged you and I whispered in your ear, *when I'm able to feel feelings again, they're all yours*—and the man standing in the elevator with us overheard, and smiled to himself and looked at his shoes, and knew he'd seen something strange?

II.

My dearest V—,

Was it only in my imagination that you trembled, my darling, ever so faintly, when I spoke her name—when I told you how *close* we'd become? You traced your fork round your plate as the blood flushed your lips. I dared not look at you too long, darling, lest you saw that I *knew...*

Just later, with a cigarette in your hand, it seemed that you yourself wanted to have a little thrill, to hide in plain sight, as you talked about meeting her—even as the mother of your children fluttered around you like a moth. You sat on the windowsill and kicked your feet.

(Of course I can't imagine that it's easy, my darling, to live your life— and isn't it you, more than anyone, that needs to *misbehave...*)

Did you wonder—even as you assured yourself of the contrary—did you wonder whether she had told me? Did you wonder whether I, with a couple of words, could unravel your life—just like that? Was it part of the *pleasure*, my darling, to wonder? Did you very nearly invite it, when, apropos of nothing, you spoke of what a marvel she was, when she appeared from out of thin air at our little fête, those few years ago?

You could not imagine, of course—even in the depth of your misgivings, you could not *fathom*—that I was writing to her at that very moment, that I was describing for her the fear and the shamelessness shining together in your eyes.

And why not, my darling, and why not. *Live.* You are now my secret, even as she is yours. You are now my plaything.

III.

My dearest E—,

Do you remember, my darling, how we were both of us naked at the cabin on the hill, with only the dog, the bookshelves on the walls, the copper pots, the little observatory we found, the grass that went on and on in every direction, the soundless sunset, the sky on fire—and, eventually, the night that enveloped it all?

IV.

My dearest E—,

What is this? Really: what *is* this?

What is this moment? This feeling? These people? These cities rising from the earth like wildgrass? How can there be so many *things*—histories, forms, ideas, sacraments? What is it that we are experiencing? This desire, this pleasure, this awe? Is not our very *capacity* for feeling shattering? I am in tears as I write you, darling. I am in tears, I am in tears, I am in tears, I am in tears.

I've been going for walks at the cemetery at the Place Gambetta. It's so pretty here, when the sun shines on the dead, on the broken rows of tombs, on the autumn trees. Here are all these people, these years, these lives we'll never know, the colossus of the human sprawl. Here are monuments to great men, and in their shadow simple markers that read, *Mon grand amour*—a letter from the living to the dead, from a single soul to another.

My darling, my love: does it not move you?

If I die, will you engrave the years of my birth and death on a headstone, and just next to it, engrave the year of your birth—and join me in a while? Have you seen the leaves shiver, just slightly, against the cloudless sky—have you felt how alive the earth is? It wears away the stone, it crumbles the tombs, until the family names have been erased. And isn't it the very liveness of the earth that buries, that *eats up* the dead?

I walk along the little lanes, beneath the maples grown so tall in time, and I see the rays of sun behind the grand, elysian structure that holds the ashes, and I keep walking, the grief of veiled women ringing in my ears, until the sun, at last, is no longer hidden by the ash-house, until it is full in my eyes, until it is in my mouth as I open it, darling—to *gasp*.

V.

Wow. Wow. Wow. Wow. Wow. Wow. Wow. Wow. Wow. Wow. Wow.
Wow. Wow. Wow. Wow. Wow. Wow. Wow. Wow. Wow. Wow. Wow.
Wow. Wow. Wow. Wow. Wow. Wow. Wow. Wow. Wow. Wow. Wow.
Wow. Wow. Wow. Wow. Wow. Wow. Wow. Wow. Wow. Wow. Wow.
Wow. Wow. Wow. Wow. Wow. Wow. Wow. Wow. Wow. Wow. Wow.
Wow. Wow. Wow. Wow. Wow. Wow. Wow. Wow. Wow. Wow. Wow.
Wow. Wow. Wow. Wow. Wow. Wow. Wow. Wow. Wow. Wow. Wow.
Wow. Wow. Wow. Wow. Wow. Wow. Wow. Wow. Wow. Wow. Wow.
Wow. Wow. Wow. Wow. Wow. Wow. Wow. Wow. Wow. Wow. Wow.
Wow. Wow. Wow. Wow. Wow. Wow. Wow. Wow. Wow. Wow. Wow.
Wow. Wow. Wow. Wow. Wow. Wow. Wow. Wow. Wow. Wow. Wow.
Wow. Wow. Wow. Wow. Wow. Wow. Wow. Wow. Wow. Wow. Wow.
Wow. Wow. Wow. Wow. Wow. Wow. Wow. Wow. Wow. Wow. Wow.
Wow. Wow. Wow. Wow. Wow. Wow. Wow. Wow. Wow. Wow. Wow.
Wow. Wow. Wow. Wow. Wow. Wow. Wow. Wow. Wow. Wow. Wow.
Wow. Wow. Wow. Wow. Wow. Wow. Wow. Wow. Wow. Wow. Wow.
Wow. Wow. Wow. Wow. Wow. Wow. Wow. Wow. Wow. Wow. Wow.
Wow. Wow. Wow. Wow. Wow. Wow. Wow. Wow. Wow. Wow. Wow.
Wow. Wow. Wow. Wow. Wow. Wow. Wow. Wow. Wow. Wow. Wow.
Wow. Wow. Wow. Wow. Wow. Wow. Wow. Wow. Wow. Wow. Wow.
Wow. Wow. Wow. Wow. Wow. Wow. Wow. Wow. Wow. Wow. Wow.
Wow. Wow. Wow. Wow. Wow. Wow. Wow. Wow. Wow. Wow. Wow.
Wow. Wow. Wow. Wow. Wow. Wow. Wow. Wow. Wow. Wow. Wow.
Wow. Wow. Wow. Wow. Wow. Wow. Wow. Wow. Wow. Wow. Wow.
Wow. Wow. Wow. Wow. Wow. Wow. Wow. Wow. Wow. Wow. Wow.
Wow. Wow. Wow. Wow. Wow. Wow. Wow. Wow. Wow. Wow. Wow.
Wow. Wow. Wow. Wow. Wow. Wow. Wow. Wow. Wow. Wow. Wow.
Wow. Wow. Wow. Wow. Wow. Wow. Wow. Wow. Wow. Wow. Wow.
Wow. Wow. Wow. Wow. Wow. Wow. Wow. Wow. Wow. Wow. Wow.
Wow. Wow. Wow. Wow. Wow. Wow. Wow. Wow. Wow. Wow. Wow.
Wow. Wow. Wow. Wow. Wow. Wow. Wow. Wow. Wow. Wow. Wow.
Wow. Wow. Wow. Wow. Wow. Wow. Wow. Wow. Wow. Wow. Wow.
Wow. Wow. Wow. Wow. Wow. Wow. Wow. Wow. Wow. Wow. Wow.
Wow. Wow. Wow.

VI.

My little love,

I saw you today, in reverie. I turned you into a color: yellow, a soft yellow-red that was like the sun shining on my closed eyes. You—your color—grew and grew from a pinpoint, you filled my body, you filled the room, the house, the yard, the yards for miles around—you filled the rivers. And I was smiling, I could hardly keep myself from *laughing out loud*, darling, having filled the world with you.

I opened my eyes and stepped onto the balcony and looked across the lawn. And I found you, rocking on your swing, your flowered dress trailing behind you, and you looked up at me and asked, *Daddy, am I still beautiful?*

VII.

To the girl seated next to me at dinner at the wedding in Voilebleu,

You told me that your father was a double agent, an operator, and you found out on his deathbed when he reconciled with your brother, with whom he'd been estranged since forbidding him to fraternize with a boy that, it turned out, was flagged in the system. He told your brother, *forgive me, but I did that because your friend was flagged in the system, and I am in fact an intelligence operator, and here I lay dying.* Etc.

And then, you told me, things began to make sense, little things like having to leave the house very suddenly in your childhood, when you were a precocious girl with excellent marks. Later your mother would tell you about the night she spent in the bathtub with a nuclear bomb: and that's when I figure you've made the whole thing up. Which was so *endearing*, darling—you were either crazy or out for a laugh, weren't you?

(When I asked you about it you laughed in this very lavish, this very rich, way—you said the wine was a bit corked, and you knew wine...)

You broke your spine climbing out of a window—you said you wanted to get down faster, that everything was like that in those days. You fell and you couldn't feel anything, you knew straight away, they picked you up and they told you that you wouldn't walk again. And here I leaned closer, because I sensed you would divulge something: a feeling, a real feeling. And I said—*how did that feel, when they told you that—really?*

And you said you were more afraid than you'd ever been in your life, more afraid than you've ever been since. But you're walking now, though you have to pee standing up, leaning with one hand on the wall like a man—and you're happy, you say, as a clam, and it was all for the best.

Marvelous, my darling. What a show.

VIII.

My dearest L—,

Another winter has passed. Another year. I've tried to tell you about my sense of awe—but what is awe to you, who already *feels* so much? You must, in some sense, find me a tourist.

There's a rush of wind at our little park, and a thousand elm seeds are falling from the treetops, spinning delicately on their axes, the city radiant, blooming, growing over itself as it's always done, while we've been halfway across the world. How could I tell you that it's not that I didn't want to live here—I just didn't want to live here with you?

I went walking downtown and I saw the kids, singing, holding hands at the bars, wearing our colors, and I thought, aren't they lucky, and weren't we them—and aren't we still? But it's someone else's turn to be young, my darling.

Do you remember, the night before I left, listening to my father's music, with the letter you would give me in your pocket? It always knocks me over when that song goes, *ti takoy khoroshiy bila*—you were so good—and it's meant as goodbye.

I told you then that I was sorry, for whatever was to come. Because you were good, my darling. You were.

IX.

My dearest R—,

On a balcony at four in the morning we're both high, as high as we've ever been, and I tell you that I love who you've become, who you're still becoming, who she made you into and what you've done with it, your face made up with cherry glitter and wearing your golden pantalon, your machismo and self-doubt softened, made fluid, reserved for jokes, ones you tell with skill.

You say you're bi, a drug addict, a Catholic—in that order. You're beginning to like how it sounds, and you know very well it sounds interesting, *whimsical* even—like the nymph of modernity in three words. You hear it, you're fine with that 'being all there is,' you know well there is more.

Do they really know you, where you go, what you *allow yourself*, at your job where you put on a suit and talk about the markets? Or do you have a compartment, a little pocket, for each of you? What if the BBC were to find you wearing eye shadow, or looking closely at a stranger's vagina at a retreat for self-reclamation?

E. told me you're sweet, and I never thought about you that way, but she's right, you *are* sweet, you are like the rest of them desperate to feel something, to *journey to the end of the night* (to borrow loosely, to bastardize Céline)—but in a more academic, in a more self-aware way— and you're sweet, my darling, you positively are.

You put your arms around me and you say, *I could go on exactly like this, losing my mind, having pretty conversations for weeks. I could annihilate myself with pretty conversations.*

X.

To the newborn daughter of my dearest W—,

My darling, your mother made the most perfectly innocent remark to me the other day: she said, she never tries to put on a show in conversation, she never wants to take too much space—if anything, she wants people to underestimate her.

Wonderful, wonderful, you might think—she is meager, she wishes to be revealed in layers, she is full of humility. But she went on to say: *like this I can catch them in their presumptions. Like this I can catch them making a mistake.*

My darling, I realized then, as your mother laughed in the most perfectly adorable way, as she asked us, *right? Do you know what I mean?* and twirled her hair round her finger—I realized then that she was fear itself—charming, yes, but fear itself.

XI.

My dearest F—,

Do they mistake your happiness for frivolity? Are they afraid that they can't make happiness out of nothing, as you can—are they intimidated? Do they believe that there isn't any room for them, in all your happiness —are they right?

You dance with your arms stretched out to either side, you dance with your neck swaying. You look like a long-body car from the 50s, like a Cadillac Eldorado with marine blue tailfins, when you dance. I can picture you at my wedding in a feather headdress, dancing like that. I can picture you on the table of the apartment we shared, wearing a jacket made of diamonds, dancing like that.

And but yet you're *delicate*, you always have been, haven't you darling? You're so often out of sorts, doubled over, sweating in your bedsheets, missing appointments, dinner parties, and the doctors can't tell why...

And I am tempted to ask: are you not, in your duality, in your grace and your affliction, the suggestion—and even the proof—of *design*? Is it that you're *paying*, darling, for your happiness? And why should you have to pay, and *who* are you paying—who made the world that way? Have you ever thought that there is no reason, really, why it can't just all be—fine?

Are you not yourself the very proof, then, that there is a god?

XII.

My dearest O—,

Haven't you sat in the car, my darling, while we've gone to pick peaches?

Haven't you pulled the car over to the side of the road, suddenly, halfway down the seashore, to phone the doctor's office and say, *hello, hello Johnny, yes, how are you, it's Mrs. —. Would you tell her please that I need her to call me—right away?*

Haven't you called us, after we'd already sat down, after we'd begun to wonder where you were, to tell us that you felt unwell—to tell us that, to your regret, you wouldn't be joining us?

Haven't you told us, *go ahead, I'll catch up with you in a while?* And you washed your hands, and perfumed your hair, and drew the curtains closed, and drifted as through a dream...

Haven't you little interest left in crowds, little patience for words without meaning, for things not going as you'd like? Haven't you grown fond, my darling, of your ghosts?

And haven't you abruptly left the Tour de la Rêverie when, at security, they asked you to open your purse? Even as your sister gave you that look—the one that says, *no, no you won't*—and, eventually, *please— please don't?*

Here's what happened next: we rode the elevator up without you and she smoothed her dress with her hands and played it all over in her mind. We reached the top and looked down over the railing—and, far below, *there you were*, my darling. Right as rain.

XIII.

My dearest P—,

When you saw me you shouted my name, you crossed the bar with your arms, your hands reaching, you took me by both shoulders—and you *shook* me. I was so glad to see you, darling. Know that you've crossed my mind more times than I can count, throughout all these years.

When we sat down together, finally, in the little room I'd rented for the weekend, the sun had begun to rise over the spires of the old town, and I drew the curtains closed, and for a moment, a single strand of light cut across your eye, your lips, your fingers tapping on your knee. And I saw that you looked worn out, darling. You looked like Adam, the first man —you looked like you were *sorry for how it had all turned out.*

For everything that had touched, that had hardened you—the things you'd said, things you found out when you opened little drawers, when you looked in their shoeboxes, when you read over their shoulders what they thought of you, how they *talked about you.* For everything that you'd accepted. It's hard to imagine that life can happen to you—to you like all of us—as the birthday cards say, *slowly and then all at once.* Isn't it? You told me that you wanted to disappear, to dig a hole clear to the other side of the world, and come up breathing the bitter air, with nobody *expecting* anything. Will you?

You've developed a sentimentality that you admit, but view with suspicion—a sentimentality that you say you're just *trying on.* And then here we are, in an alternate timeline or on an island in time, and you say, *couldn't we have been happy?* But it's easy when it's new again.

XIV.

My dearest N—,

I ask you what it's like to be you, and you tell me that it's grand, really—it's lovely. And come to think of it, you, with all your anxieties, you with all your *dread*—you are all in all quite *sure* of yourself, aren't you? And you come from fine stock, at least the second generation that can tell a hell of a story with a drink in your hand, that can send a heartfelt note of thanks from the taxi home (you're so good at goodbyes, darling—one of the best I've ever seen). No, my darling, I suppose the fault you see in the world lies in others, not in how you see yourself.

I tell you about something I read in a book: a young man sits with his mother as she's dying. And they've never really talked—I mean they've talked, of course, but not about *what it's like to be him*, how it *feels*. I suppose a lot of mothers come and go without getting that from their sons, and sons without telling their mothers.

You talk to your mother all the time, don't you—you open another bottle and you talk? Yes, you tell me, you talk—but not *really*. And I start thinking that, when I look at photos of my little girl when she was younger, still a baby, she looks like she's someone else—that I just can't *remember* her that way. I remember, intellectually, but I don't *feel* the memory, can you see what I mean? Or when I think about her then, I substitute her as she is right now, all grown up, an older double for herself.

And so if that's how it is, do our mothers lose us as children—even in their memory—and do they never come to know us as adults—and what should we tell them before they die?

I sometimes feel like it could be the last time I see you, darling. My father said it, when we last got together with our relatives: he said, *maybe, this is the last time*. And he gave a toast: not his best, just effortless and touching. I'd already felt that way at my wedding—who had I seen *for the last time*—friends, relatives, people that once mattered to me—though neither of us knew it? And maybe that's alright, maybe we had our day. And it was good, or it was all that we could do.

XV.

My dearest H—,

And what about me—should I say a few words? I've given you so little —I've hardly *confessed* to you at all. That's suited me of course, darling. I haven't minded you saying how mysterious I am, how unknowable. I've spoken of myself in the abstract, I've described someone that could be me, or is very nearly me. Even when I've told you, darling, in all my earnestness, of what's moved me—even when I told you of what's buried me. Did you have the impression, then—that I've told you nothing at all?

You asked me if I trust the universe, if I trust it will all be alright in the end. I told you, my darling, that I hardly trust another person to fill the silence...

In truth, darling, in truth I am terrified of the silence, and I view it as a deeply, as an entirely *personal* failing. Does it not pain you, too—the silence? The mundanity? Doesn't it need some flash—some provocation? Some subversion? Some specter of the *provocateur*? And if we can't have that, my darling—if I can't give it to you, if I cannot make things more *interesting* for you, if I cannot find the words...

Of course I want you—and why not you most of all—to find me beautiful, to be charmed—perhaps even to *enjoy yourself*. Would the whores, for their part, not be saved, not be *transported*, when it's me at the door —and not someone else? Would that not give them some *relief*? And so may it be for you, and so why not show you, make you well aware, of my particular—talents?

And so what about me—should I say a few words? Here is a description: clever, beautiful, subversive—provocative. That is how I would have you see me, though inside I'm rotten, rotting—perhaps much more than you, much more than anyone—rotting from the burning fear, the *terror*, that you won't cede the floor so I can do my tricks, that you won't clap when I take a bow...

If I dare to have an original thought, and it isn't any good, then am I not like the acrobat that has no business on the stage? And if I define myself with the original thought, am I not, then—nothing? They say that the difference between the artist and the neurotic, who are both obsessed, is nothing other than talent...

(Are you surprised when I tell you how self-conscious I am—how I'm always playing a part, always wondering how I've come off? Do you believe me? And what of this self-revelation, this *confession*? Does it draw you in all the more? Does it make me more human, does it make you forgive me—does it make you want me more?)

You once told me, *you just want to love people*—I quickly corrected you, *I just want them to love me*. And so of course I am always assuring people at parties that I'm not aloof—I am, rather, deathly afraid.

But that's not what I tell you, darling, is it? I tell you that in certain circles, I mean amongst a small number of people who *get it*—well, they must find me rather remarkable—they must find me rather *impressive*. And it's very important that they feel this way and that they tell me their secrets, one after the other. That they feel they are the only one in the world. And they are, and they are. I am afraid of disappointing them. For I love and esteem them truly, and I want to ask them about their jobs, and their children, and what embarrasses them—though I can never keep what they've told me for myself.

XVI.

My dearest B—,

When the fire service comes to pick you up you're sitting on the floor and you look up at them and cradle yourself tenderly in your own arms and you ask, *why do I have to go?* And they answer that it's because you've admitted that you no longer want to *live*, my darling—and we've got to do something about that, haven't we? The blood is drying on your father's forehead, and in your fingernails.

And it's funny, isn't it, all this—that we, the living, send men who will command you: *live*. There are perhaps ten of them, speaking in hushed voices of authority. Big, strong men, all—ready for you to *flee*. They would catch you by the collar of your shirt, my darling, just as if you were a wisp of cotton... Because if you did it—if you went and killed yourself—well, you might come to regret it, eventually—don't you think?

Your mother called this morning in a panic: you wouldn't get out of bed to take your exam. Although your very life depended on it—*because* your life depended on it. E. went over and threw water in your face and told you that you're going, you're going and that's all there is to it. She's good at that kind of thing. But I understand your dread, darling. If we would admit our impotence before the terror of nature, before death that comes for us all, before the sheer unlikelihood, the seeming impossibility of our hero-project, the rarity of heroes, the multitudes upon multitudes of *failed men*—before these staggering odds, before their consequence, which is to render us meaningless—I can understand you. We are the rest of us crazy, not you.

XVII.

My dearest S—,

You've written me a few times now—you've sent me photos of your life: here is the view from my office, here is my fiancé, here is the park where we go for walks. I haven't written you back, as if nothing had ever happened between us, as if we hadn't been kids together—as if we'd never been *close*. As if I don't think of you, when I think of me, in that place and in that time—as if I wasn't happy to have you there, happy to have a friend of my own. I suppose, my darling, that the truth is, I just don't see *the point* in telling you how I've been. But that's not fair. I take walks now, too—I started today.

What was it like—to stay there? While everything changed, while Brooklyn became Bethlehem—while it became *New York*? Who did you become? Everyone we knew never amounted to much, did they?

Remember we used to whisper to each other at night, lying awake in the dark? You were on your way, then—you were ready to *crack*. Could I have saved you? Of course, I would have willingly *become* you, if my constitution had allowed it. How many lives you've had, my darling. I hope you left it all behind—really. I did.

XVIII.

My dearest E—,

I see your face in the rearview mirror—

driving through the cornfields, looking out the window with your city dress on.

And the song on the radio goes, *you're the first, you're the last, my everything*.

And you start to smile, and you turn away from the window. And your eyes look for mine.

XIX.

My dearest E—,

How can you do that? To go on, when everything is falling apart, just as if it wasn't? To laugh on the phone, to hang paintings on the walls—to give instructions to the men who work for you?

You will remember Hemingway's *dust*, his many references to *dusty roads*, trampled by armies. Don't you go and go until you are, yourself, Hemingway's dusty roads, trod by armies, the dust settling onto the leaves of the trees as into the creases of your hands, into the grooves around your eyes? Here is your lifeforce, the titan walls of your soul.

You tell me sometimes, *if I stop moving, I'll fall over and I won't get up again*. (And haven't I seen it, when you finally collapse in bed, and you cannot for the life of you rise, and you ask, you beg, to be *served...*) I suppose that's it, my darling. I suppose that's what's *got you all this*.

But don't you ask what's happening to us, as if you haven't had a hand in it—as if you haven't tipped the scale. Is that how you stay upright? Have you absolved yourself—haven't you gone to sing to yourself in the garden? Certainly your conviction holds you. Certainly you believe in your core that you may not be innocent, but you are, all in all, *right...*

And if you'll permit me to say, my darling, I've screamed and screamed in the car, driving alone through the cornfields.

XX.

My dearest Q—,

You tell me that you have this utterly boring habit of kissing things that you love.

You tell me, doesn't the word *douceur*, in French, sound like your head hitting the pillow—the feeling, yes, but also the sound?

You tell me, *I love the moon and the sun. God knows that when I was 5, I told them that they are my parents.* And all the stars were your sisters.

You tell me that you wanted to be a dentist when you grew up. You loved going to the dentist—the comfortable chair, the warm light, the *rosy little mouth germ* in the book he gave you. You tell me, *you wanted to be an astronaut? How common.*

You tell me that you've never understood these girls that wear necklaces with their names written in gold letters, their own names hanging around their necks, names like Kimberly or Ashley.

You tell me, *I'm always browsing for the best hotels in Haiti, or Afghanistan—in war zones, in failed states.* Just to see what it's like...

You tell me, your guilt does not inspire you to make any grand gestures, does not inspire you to make gifts that they will never know were given as atonement. You simply sleep with your mouth open in the car.

You tell me, *it was just one of those things, darling, without any ontology.* Without any reason. Without any care.

But you've got tears in your eyes again: aren't we beautiful? Hadn't we nearly—vanished?

You tell me that you call it, *3 days on LSD and a sunset in Pennsylvania.*

XXI.

My dearest C—,

I tell you that I'm writing a book of poetry, so you think it over and you look at me and you say, *well then, tell me something poetic.* I tell you, *it's going to be ok. You're going to be ok.* You tell me that's not poetry—that's a fortune cookie. And you grab the vodka from my hand and you announce that you don't want to go home, and you take a long, hard drink. And then you start to choke, and you run to the bathroom and I can hear you retching and when you come back I realize that you've vomited blood. That you've got blood on your face, on your hands. That you're sick, my darling—that you can't help yourself.

I won't give you the bottle after that, I keep it away from you with one hand, and with my other hand I take your wrist and ask you to let me call you a cab. You push me away and you run for the bar, you unscrew a bottle of wine and you take another drink, you get blood on the bedsheets, you pour the rest of the bottle down the sink, you scream for me to keep my fucking hands off you, you scream that I don't care, you scream that I'm a coward. And all at once, you disappear into the night, leaving your socks.

I clean the blood off the bathroom floor with toilet paper and I think of how, while we were talking, for a while you didn't want it to end, you asked if I could follow you to the bathroom while you peed, so we wouldn't have to end it even for a second.

And then after a long while, darling, I manage to sleep. And here is what I dream: that you're holding me, telling me it's too soon for you to die. You're squeezing me so tight I'm afraid you'll break the bones in your fingers. And before you leave this world, you give me the performance of what you'd done—the *spectacle* of it. Of the blood and the socks and all. You give me what's left of you.

And when I wake up I ache for you, I am in awe of you, I wish that I could be so fragile, I wish that I could want as you want, I wish I could drop to my knees before you—but I'm learning, darling. I'm learning to care.

XXII.

My dearest G—,

When you left your husband and came to do bêtises with us, to live as we were living, between one salon and another, you adapted so very well, darling—I mean that you committed, didn't you, to the role? After 10 years, more, playing the good wife, you became someone else, or you became yourself, you were always out and everyone wanted you and you wanted them and you took everything they had to give. And you had a hard time with it after a while, you felt too far gone and doubtless you were right, you were not only on the scene but you were also ruining yourself, your work, your attachments, you were voracious, you were a child again. And what I will always admire is that, when it caught up to you, when you did, finally, *go too far*, I thought you would say, *I was lost, les amours,* and *don't I know it.* But instead you told us—if you'll please forgive my paraphrasing—*it is not for you, my absolution* and *I'll live this way for one more day or for a lifetime.* And you disappeared, my darling, just as quickly as you'd come to know us, even as we sent you photos from the seashore.

XXIII.

To the girl that sat across from me on the 12:14 to Deauville,

What gave you goosebumps, as you looked out the train window? You didn't notice, but the way you looked, lost in your thoughts, I thought I'd better take your photograph. Have you ever supposed, my darling, that we could, any of us, be hanging somewhere on a wall? That a stranger could find in us something—*universal*?

XXIV.

My dearest Z—,

And you, and you my darling—after all this time, you've still got that air, that suggestion, that if you're pushed, really pushed, all your love will unravel, layer by layer—the way you take someone's arm, put your head on their shoulder, smile and ask *how they're doing, really*—it will all peel away to reveal that inside, you are cold, you are up for anything, and nothing could surprise you—that you've insulated yourself, that you never flinch at the dark, the vaudeville, the fantasies of men. I know with certainty that you watch yourself moving from above, that you observe yourself acting in society, and you are very careful that nobody ever knows, nobody ever begins to *suspect*, how detached you are. How in other circumstances, not so very different than these, you wouldn't mind sinking your teeth into their neck...

XXV.

My dearest U—,

I'm thinking again of the Château de la Rose, of the red disco lights streaked across your face, of your shirt undone, of the devil in your eyes. In those days, you were ready to feel something, darling, you were dangerous, weren't you?

You took people aside, strangers, and they told you everything, everything, they *confessed* to you, and you swallowed them whole, you strung their memories up like garlands, you told them sincerely that you loved them.

Do you remember how *the one for you* came singing, crawling, meowing down the marble staircase at midnight? How she had announced herself with an Indian war-cry and a fox fur coat? How she crawled on her knees to the piano and began to play, beautifully, like grace, how you kept saying, *c'est qui cette fille, c'est qui cette fille, c'est qui cette fille, c'est qui cette fille?*

You pulled her over to dance and the disco lights went streaking across her hair...

Would you believe, my darling, that for all of that, for all the *run* you were on—what it makes me think of most is that I miss it? That I miss you, us? Why'd you go and burn up out there? Why'd you go and do that?

Let me imagine you as you want me, as you want us, to imagine you: at the last Carrefour before the front line, packing your shopping cart, hungry, insatiable, because they could at any moment kill you dead.

XXVI.

My dearest X—,

I remember I saw you at our café in the meat district. That was more than a decade ago, that was four years after I left, and it was like I never had, and we were closer to that summer, then, than we are to our lives, now—do you know what I mean?—and you hadn't changed, you told me, *God, it feels exactly the same, doesn't it*—and you looked at me in wonder, and later you left me at the train station and I exhaled. I stood there at the tracks and just breathed.

I'd seen a ghost, I'd almost followed you home, and really, I left you there, I saw you again years later but that wasn't you, you didn't have much to tell me, you were resigned to your life in that little college town, it was boring but the people were kind and the walks were good—but I won't remember you like that, my darling.

And aren't the wheat fields of France, browning in the summer, beautiful—how they cut them around the islets of forest—and didn't you read about them, didn't you want a chance to see them—and to see, of course, Paris? I hope you'll visit, and see the fields rolling around Paris, and the islets, the way they look in the morning from a train window.

It's funny—are you listening?—I too have seen moments of fate. Of when it all gets decided (but you realize after, only after). When at Go-Go in the meat district (they've closed it now) a girl grabbed my hand and pulled me into a dance circle and into the life, then and there, of her best friend... and if you froze that moment, and then accelerated time, and you watched the arrow of her life (the best friend), now she—now you—have a nail shop in that little college town. What if I were a foot away?

XXVII.

To the *it girl* of Kyiv,

How did you end up?

I'm thinking of the little moments—the tragedies, yes—but also the countless ordinary, even pretty moments, the arcs of people's lives bent in funny ways, intersecting as the city writhes—the lovers who first meet in the metro stations when the air raid sirens come on, the artists who are discovered when television crews come to film the apartment blocks on fire.

I'm thinking of what became, of what becomes, of you, the society girl, one of the beautiful people. Who helps you, who falls for you, what's your story? Is it very different, darling, than the rest—for all your *power*? What do you cause to happen? What happens to charismatic people during the war?

Can I tell you what I once saw at the cemetery? A small grave, an ordinary grave, an ordinary life—but it was covered, darling, absolutely covered, in plastic flowers, and it was covered with plaques, and one of the plaques read, *to my diva—to my goddess*, and they'd etched an image of a woman onto it, in black and white, and she had such fine hair, she looked proud—she looked electric. She'd spent not 35 years on Earth, but how they *remembered* her.

Forgive me, we are strangers. How will they memorialize you, beauty queen?

<h1 style="text-align:center">XXVIII.</h1>

My dearest V—,

You told me, as we sat at the courtyard at the Rue de l'Ailleurs, that there was some part of you that would never, could never, belong to her, and that that was alright, that was the natural course of things—though we were speaking of betrayal, though we were speaking of how you *justified what you'd done*, darling—and you looked up in all oblivion at the buildings, like you'd said the most obvious thing in the world, like the matter was so explained—and closed—and I thought, staring at those buildings that were *witness*, that it sounds fine when you put it like that, and it even sounds reasonable, but people are everything but reasonable, darling, and it was all everything but fine...

XXIX.

To the springtime lover of my dearest K—,

Your editor tells you that the way you've written it—*in what we learn about you in this piece*—you don't seem to have done it, have you—you haven't actually come to embody your notions of *libertinism*? Your editor tells you, *he is the one with a lover for each finger, not you*—and you, my darling, agreed for him to find a finger for you.

What have you said about him, I wonder, in your diary? How have you described him? Yourself in his reflection? And how it all turns out? Someone told me today something to the effect of, *and that's the work—talking about it.* We talk and talk and talk and talk, and then the revelation—and then we find out how we really *feel*—isn't that it?

Do you feel that you are attracted to polyamory because no one wants you entirely? Do you think, with condescension—do you allow yourself this—that he's better off with you, but has yet to admit it, even to himself?

Do you remember, at dinner, when I told you I felt lost, and you shook me and said, *well then we have to look for you, we have to look for you, we have to look for you*? I took you trembling in my arms because you were, you were again, beside yourself.

XXX.

My dearest A—,

I'll teach you about the world—your mother will teach you how to live in it, darling. Somewhere along the way, you'll ask yourself: and so what matters, truth or feeling? The answer, I suppose, my darling, is that neither matters very much—though remark that there is much ado about truth. Remark that all we ever experience is feeling. Your mother has a *capacity* for feeling that the rest of us cannot begin to imagine...

But I am so happy for you to ask the question—I'm so *afraid* for you, darling. Always be in awe, always ask: how can it be that this, this now, is happening—how can it be that I'm here to see it? And: aren't I lucky?

You are clever, darling, and if you let your cleverness lead you into cynicism you will always be alone. If you intellectualize everything you will miss the thing-in-itself, the naked filament, the living wire—you will miss touching it directly, darling, and then you will deny your humanity, or you will think your humanity away.

If nothing matters, if I am made of matter, then how can I feel longing? But the tension is between feeling and reason, feeling and knowing— not between feeling and experience. Indeed our experience is unambiguous, in that we feel what we feel—do you understand, darling? And feeling is real, more real to us than what we measure with our instruments. And if nothing matters anyway, if we are made of matter anyway, then the truth is only a thing to amuse, to stimulate, ourselves—but feeling, we should take seriously. We may even dare to take feeling as truth —why jump through hoops? Here in front of you, is feeling. Do you accept it?

(Your mother would say it's neither about feeling nor truth, but about love...)

But with that said—let no one reduce us to conductor rods, darling, that wait for lightning to strike. Let no one reduce us to feeling alone. Let no one tell you that the human mind is anything less than inspired. Let no one tell you that man is anything less than God. Here is what I mean:

31

Did you know, my darling, that the way we discover new kinds of stars is we pick up their signature with a telescope, we plot the pattern of light that they emit on a graph, and we draw something like this (this is a star): ⋀ . And we look at it and say: *this is a new kind of star, we haven't seen one like this before*. It will remind you, darling, of how we observe the heart, the brain, the breath...

And here's what's unbelievable: with lines on paper, we can correctly describe an unfathomably alien object, billions of light years away, born before our own moon—and perhaps, by the time we see it, already dead. We can know nearly everything there *is* to know about it. We can study it and write textbooks about it, we can have symposiums about its strange properties—as we can about the heart itself. Pause a moment, darling, to think about it.

A person, we have seen, is a universal explainer: a computational system with infinite reach. A person can explain what the sky is made of. Look in the sky at Jupiter, at Saturn, at the Sun, all of the stars—how grand they are. But you can go there, darling, in your mind's eye you can walk their surface, you can leap from one to another in a flash, with no suit, with no capsule—you can imagine their destruction, you can envision their creation, you can travel beyond them, travel so far that they, each so grand, each a leviathan in its own part of space—are forgotten, are unknown. And we could posit that in your brain there is more complexity, in a single nerve firing, than in the furnace of the sun, than in the storms of Jupiter—even more than in the largest storm, the eye of Jupiter, that is larger than the Earth.

And doesn't the infinite appear here, here in this life—here on earth? In the possibility—in the action potential—of the human experience—in all of the things that may happen—in all of the ways it might *turn out*? Each human is a product of some esoteric combinatorics, of genetic and epigenetic expression, geography, circumstance, fate, action, choice. And couldn't any sufficiently talented man change his life with a few words— if he could just say the right words, in the right order, to the right people? And isn't that, too, some kind of combinatorics—do we not construct sentences that move people, as biology constructs life that *lives*?

And what of all these people, masses upon masses of them, each a closed conduit for and of their own experience, each with a unique past, a childhood, a coming of age, capabilities, needs, dreams, a routine, a place to sleep, people to love, things to do, a point of view, a continuity—what happened a moment ago, what happens now, what will happen in a moment—a humanity that isn't ours, that we cannot know—that we cannot *conceive of*? All of these people living in their own bodies, having only this life—for better and for worse? The permutations of existence —and the inability to try on another existence, or even to know much of anything about the lives, in their fullness (they are, after all, *lives*!) of our contemporaries, let alone the dead and those yet unborn—isn't this what the mind was made to contemplate?

How can it be that other people's stories, that you didn't yourself experience, are true—are real? If we can access the universe only through the mind—if experience is, in this sense, not just local but entirely confined —is not that experience, then, the universe itself—for isn't the universe defined as being *all there is*? And so, even if corroborated by witnesses and evidence, are other people's stories anything more than images and sound in your mind—are they anything more than films? What you experience is real—what I experience is only real as far as you see and hear me tell you about it—is that not what the notion of a universe implies? Don't I need to conjure the entire universe to conjure you—or anyone else?

You will hear people call people ugly. You will hear people call people a virus. But perhaps the spacemen, those that are far more advanced than we are, those that have eliminated greed, violence, and otherness from society, those that are *enlightened*—perhaps they look at us and think, not that we are ugly, but rather that we are beautiful, that our flaws and our striving make us beautiful. Perhaps they think that we are not in some transition state, but that we are the ideal. In all our squalor. In all our hate. In all our capacity to feel.

And in any case, darling—if everything is changing, anything goes, doesn't it? Some few hundred years ago, a child expected to live the same way his parents lived, and expected his own children to live as he himself lived, and so on unto oblivion—today the world changes not on the scale of decades, nor even of years, but months, weeks, days. And so what of the underlying structures? Not only political, but normative, behavioral—the way we talk at the table, ask a girl to dance—the minutia, you see, of how we live? If the world changes, so too can we, so too should we. So: everything from first principles, then. As I've told you, my darling, think always in this way: *why are things the way they are— must they be this way—can I change it.*

Somewhere along the way, you'll ask yourself: what does it mean? The psychoanalysts have told us that we all want to realize our secret, special power—to unleash it upon the world, to become in this way heroes and to achieve immortality. They observe that during the French Revolution, the mental hospitals were empty, for every man knew his place... In terms less grand, they tell us of self-actualization, of uncovering our unconscious powers and desires and manifesting them in the psyche. They tell us that indeed, this is how we touch the infinite, and may even be the meaning of life, or at least how we *find meaning*. And maybe this is what is so intriguing about these go-getters and productive types: that they seem to be *doing that*. And if one day you've done it, darling—how can I fault you? If you do not seek—if you prefer to *be*.

But what then, of the spiritual? Did Aldous Huxley not realize, when he took mescaline in L.A. in the 50s, that there was a transcendent intricacy in the very creases of his pants?

Thousands of years from now, when the fruit of our reason frees us from the chains of survival, and from the chains, too, of *whatever it is we're living now*, we will not go into retrograde—quite the contrary, my darling—we will become sexier, more witty, better at dinner parties, better at games, we will terraform planets as we decorate our living rooms... and, finally, when we have nothing left to feel, we will sublimate into the pure information that describes our minds. And we will float, my darling, through space, humming a little tune.

XXXI.

My dearest J—,

Sometimes you're absolutely positively on-fucking-fire, the cosmic id, licking and biting and rubbing away the teeth marks, producing from your guts the sound of a woman moaning, of a cat out for sex, telling me and everyone else, the waitress, the bartender, everyone, that you love them, that you mean it, getting up on the tables and screaming it, proving it, taking off your clothes, putting on a show, a character, looking at your reflection in the window, regretting it and simultaneously wishing you had gone further, wondering if this is how people see you, if this is what you are for them, retreating inside of yourself, falling into one of your dark moods until, until finally, you shrink to a pinpoint...

And so how could anyone ever forget you?

XXXII.

My dearest I—,

I came to see you in your little house in the suburbs, with your mail-order furniture, your yard, your beautiful dogs. You were quiet, my darling, you moved delicately, as if through amber. You gave us mini-bar vodkas and ate pills from your medicine drawer and said that this was atonement, that this was the same reason your wife had gone away to the city, that you were taking it day by day. I saw flashes, darling, of who you were, of course—of who you'd *been*, underneath all that. Underneath what you'd done and the aftermath.

What a story, what a trip, though, darling, isn't it? How you'd just—dropped out. Turned up in strange places with no one knowing how you'd got there, playing blackjack, buying dancers, putting strangers up in hotel rooms, out for days on end, sweating, fevered, your eyes shot, your wife asking where you were, when you'd come home, running out of money, putting up the mortgage, calling from the casino floor to ask for a loan, absolutely sure that you would hit the big one—what they call a *manic episode*. And what an episode, my darling.

And now you're going back to work, back to surgery, and I worry that the pills they put you on have slowed your hand, if not your mind. I know that you meditate and that you cry, darling, and so do I—for in what world is such depth of sensibility, of experience, be it tragic, made possible—and cannot we be glad, after all, that it's in ours? I love you, brother. I love you, brother. I love you, brother.

XXXIII.

My dearest M—,

You asked me, with your eyes half-closed late at night and in all earnestness, if perhaps you'd been flippant about our friendship, if you've had a laugh with me but not *been there* for me.

I didn't tell you this then, but I can assure you—and I hope this will console you, though certainly it will hurt you—I can assure you that you need not worry about being much else than a *good time*, my darling. And you're perfectly amusing, you're perfect for a laugh, darling. You are.

XXXIV.

My dearest D—,

You went traveling the world and you left it all behind, your job, your cares, your ambition. You thought that you were, finally, in control of your life—you supposed that this, what you felt now, was what feeling *was*—and you watched the sunsets in California and gathered the sand in your hands and threw it in the air so that it caught the light and fell back to the ground tenderly, drifting in the wind, and you took photographs and wore love-child shawls—and I imagine that you were happy, my darling.

And there is something to that story, and the soul wants adventure, wants *pilgrimage*, doesn't it—you are neither the first nor the last, darling, you come into existence as an archetype, as a shade of what we all of us are. And hence what came next: you ran out of time, out of money, out of places to see. And you came home, though you were in your mind still wandering, still somewhere *out there*. And you refused to go back to the world you left behind, the world you thought full of pleasantries and formality and empty gestures—the world that you'd once joined, when you thought that *being someone* was more important than *feeling something*.

And so you got stuck, darling. For all your intelligence, for all your potential. You stayed home and you took care of the kids and you allowed the insults to accumulate...

And isn't your wall, at the center of your living room, a shrine, with its photographs, to what you'd done—to when you'd been alive? And can you bear to look at it, can you bear to notice it—to be transported to that time? Have you ever felt nostalgia that chokes you by the throat, that is unbearable, that is *incapacitating*? I've felt it, darling. I've had it sneak up on me.

Would you say that that sense, that *flavor* of nostalgia, when you miss something so much that you can't take it, means you're unhappy—or that you've had a good life? And have you noticed, darling, that the older we get, the more nostalgia is ever-present? How can you hang those photos on your wall?

XXXV.

To the old man who came to sing on the metro at Belleville, with a music box on wheels,

It was after I saw your wedding ring that I couldn't help myself—that I wept for you. Because you weren't very good, my darling, were you? But here you were, at the end of your life—doing what you could. What did you tell your wife, when it came down to it? *I'll get a music box and a microphone and I'll go sing on the metro, and it'll be alright.*

And don't we all of us want to be alright?

You were wearing a burgundy dinner jacket, you'd polished your shoes and put oil in your hair. You were dignified. Who am I, then, to assume that you were destitute? And how dare I imagine that you saw yourself that way—or that you *suffered* anything at all?

How inconceivably unlikely, darling, to run into you—I mean in the celestial sense. In the sense that it is always a miracle for any two living beings to cross paths in the fullness of time. I want you to know that, though my heart broke for you, what I felt most of all was how human you were, before this train car full of people, singing *Oh Yoko!* in your strange accent, just quietly over the music.

When you'd finished you went around with your little black purse, small enough to fit between your thumb and forefinger, and I saw the thin, simple gold ring you wore flash in the yellow light. And so I *wept.* I wept for your striving—I wept for your life and mine.

XXXVI.

My dearest E—,

I'd sat here, in this plaza overlooking the tubes and steel of the Centre Pompidou, a decade ago, writing in a little notebook, much like this one —and I remember thinking, it was all so grand, it was all so unlikely, it was all so new. I was living, then, in Paris, for the first time. It was spring. I was living in a little flat nearby, it was gorgeous, I was lucky, and I was starting, then, to see you...

Neither of us was the same then, as we are now, were we darling? Not really. Not really. Everything has changed now, hasn't it? Our faces, the way we see things, the way we feel, what matters, who we want to be, who we want to be *seen as*—everything has changed, hasn't it—everything but Paris. Everything but this building. This plaza. These cafés. The people even are the same—though they are different, though there are different students sitting on the cobblestones, though the gypsy men sell different rings...

I'm more pretty now than I was then. More clever. More in awe of the human condition—though less in awe of the world, less in awe of the things in it. Less full of possibility. Less hopeful, less ecstatic to find out what will happen next. More housetrained, more of a drinker, more in love with people, less in love with stories, less adventurous, more witty, more self-conscious, more reflective, more seeking, more inward.

And really the truth is, I remember the scenes, the *things*—my pen, my notebook, the plaza—more than I remember how I felt, what I thought —I remember but I don't, not really, who I *was*.

XXXVII.

My dearest E—,

You once put a notebook in my pocket in Barcelona—you'd written me a letter, in the form of a wind-up clock. It was a decade ago now (I have it in a box, a white box with little things you've given me), I was catching a plane, you told me: *read this later when I'm gone.* And then you vanished for a while, little love, didn't you?

You didn't write me that you loved me, but you wrote me all the reasons why you could, all the reasons why you very nearly did, and you wrote me that you shouldn't or you wouldn't, and you kept making note of the time, you wrote: *it's getting late*, and *soon you'll be here*, and *here you are*, and *now time is—up.* (You'd flipped the notebook over and started writing from the other end.) And you signed it, *E.*

And here we are, little love, aren't we?

What a mythos we have, little love, don't we?

E., my E., my E.! In all your power, all your fiery grace. Isn't it so that not one of our ancestors died before giving life to children, not one, in an unbroken chain since the beginning of time, when we were, all of us, fish? That the universe, the earth itself, is billions of years old, that there are billions of stars in this galaxy—that there are billions of galaxies? That the void that came before us, pales only before the void that is to follow?

I offer you the memory of a yellow rose seen at sunset, years before you were born, said Borges.

And on and on: all of the little accidents, the Slavs who came to the Haute-Marne after the war, the town fed by the river, the trees sawn into houses, your mother cooking, your father reading books, your sister laughing and smoking cigarettes, the things you dreamed in Nancy, your seven Russian winters, the silhouettes you cut from paper in London, the restlessness you felt that night, maybe every night, in Paris, when you told me to unbutton my collar, when you left me on the dance floor, when you changed your mind and reappeared to (and then, *and then*, little love...) kiss me, not knowing what it meant—how could either of

41

us have *known*. And then I let go your hand and went round the world again, and the world turned and turned on its axis.

You remember the rest, little love, don't you?

Ten years later, in our little house in the forest, there are all the disco balls, dozens of them, the ones that didn't make it to our wedding, swaying, just gently, in the wind, the doors of the sunroom open on both sides, and you can lie there and look up, just watching them as you like. And we have watched them, little love, haven't we?

You are my life, I mean you are my life itself, I mean I don't know how to separate you, to distinguish you, from the rest of it, I haven't been able to for years, I don't remember what it was like—I don't remember what *I* was like—before you, I don't exist without your seeing me, I am explained in you, I am shaped by you, or we are shaped onto each other, you filling the space that I don't, and me, in turn, filling the space around you, like leaves growing from a tree.

Doesn't the universe exist in us, through us? Haven't we no need for the universe, then, isn't that so—when we put it like that? And haven't all the moments led to this one? And don't the moments yet to come follow from here?

You're always showing up in my dreams. The other day, I dreamt of pterodactyls. In my dream, I turned to you, I said: *look—pterodactyls. Isn't that something?*

You'll write to me, won't you?